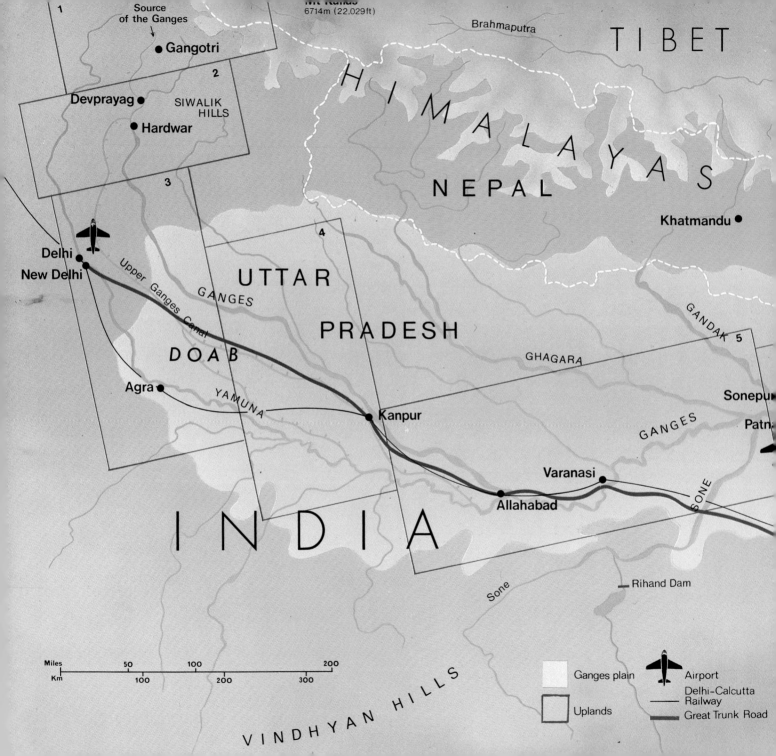

1

Source of the Ganges

● **Gangotri**

2

● **Devprayag**

SIWALIK
HILLS

● **Hardwar**

3

Mt Kailas
6714m (22,029ft)

Brahmaputra

T I B E T

H I M A L A Y A S

N E P A L

Khatmandu ●

Delhi
New Delhi

Upper Ganges Canal

GANGES

UTTAR

4

PRADESH

GHAGARA

GANDAK

5

Sonepu

DOAB

YAMUNA

Agra ●

Kanpur

GANGES

Patn

Varanasi ●

SONE

I N D I A

Allahabad ●

Sone

— Rihand Dam

Miles   50   100   200
Km   100   200   300

VINDHYAN HILLS

Ganges plain   ✈ Airport

Uplands   —— Delhi-Calcutta
                          Railway
                      ━━ Great Trunk Road

TIBET

Brahmaputra

HIMALAYAS

Mt Everest
8848m
(29,030ft)

SIKKIM

BHUTAN

NEPAL

BRAHMAPUTRA

6

INDIA

KHASI HILLS

ANGES

Monghyr

BANGLADESH 7

8

N

Farraka Barrage

PADMA (Ganges)

Meghna

Dacca

INDIA

Damodar

Bhagirathi

Garai

Calcutta

SUNDARBANS

Hooghly

Sagar Island

Bay of Bengal

A journey down the Ganges

The River Ganges starts in an ice cave high up in the Himalaya Mountains. Many Indians believe it is a sacred river.

In this book we shall take a journey from the source in the Himalayas to the mouth in the Bay of Bengal. We shall see how the river has affected people's lives. We shall also see some of the problems which India and Bangladesh have to face today.

A holy man on the bank of the Ganges

River Journeys

A journey down the Ganges

Laurie Bolwell

River Journeys

A journey up the Amazon
A journey down the Danube
A journey down the Ganges
A journey down the Mississippi
A journey up the Nile
A journey down the Rhine
A journey down the Seine
A journey down the Thames

Some words in this book are printed
in **bold**. Their meanings are explained
in the glossary on page 62.

*This book is based on an
original text by Gina Douglas*

First published in 1985 by
Wayland (Publishers) Ltd
49 Lansdowne Place, Hove
East Sussex BN3 1HF, England

© Copyright 1985 Wayland (Publishers) Ltd

ISBN 0 85078 498 0

Filmset by Latimer Trend & Company Ltd, Plymouth
Printed in Italy by G. Canale & C.S.p.A., Turin
Bound in the UK by R. J. Acford, Chichester

Contents

The Sacred River

The River Ganges starts very
high up in the Himalayas.
Many other rivers run into it.
It is not one of the world's
longest rivers but it drains
water from a huge area.
Millions of people live along
the banks of the Ganges.

The holy statue in this picture
floats near the river bank.
It is an image of Ganga, the
goddess of the Ganges.
She carries a pot of river
water in her hand.

Many Indians belong to the **Hindu** religion.
Hindu **pilgrims** come from all over India to visit the Ganges because they believe the river is sacred.
If Hindus bathe in this river their sins are washed away.
The ashes of the dead are also put in the river.

Because the river is holy its water is bottled.
Pilgrims take the holy water home with them.

These are some of the Himalaya Mountains.
They contain many of the highest peaks in the world.
They are snow-covered because they are so high.
In these mountains the rivers flow through **gorges**.
The gorges are narrow and very deep.

This diagram shows the path of the River Ganges.
The river drops sharply from the mountains to the foothills.
It rains heavily in the foothills so the rivers grow larger.
Sometimes the Ganges floods the land.
At Hardwar the River Ganges enters its long flat **plain**.
Now it flows slowly, winding from side to side.
The water looks muddy because it carries **silt**.
When the river reaches the sea it drops the silt.
The silt forms a huge **delta** in the Bay of Bengal.

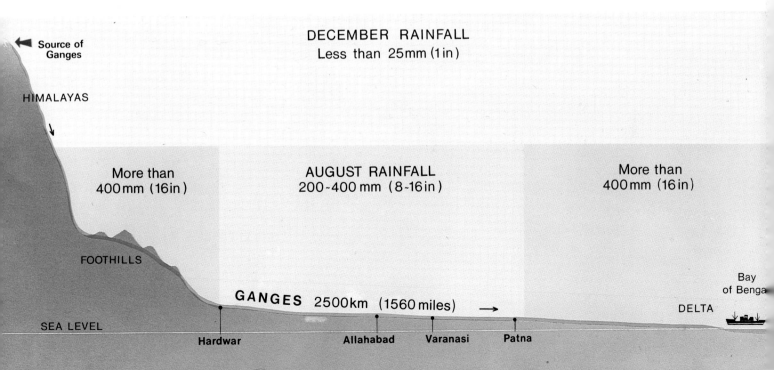

From the Ice Cave

Here is the ice cave at the source of the River Ganges.
A **saddhu**, or holy man, is walking naked in the snow.
Some holy men camp out all winter near the cave.
They bathe in the icy water every morning.

The nearest village to the ice cave is Gangotri.
Can you find it on the map?
There is a temple at Gangotri where offerings are made
to the gods.

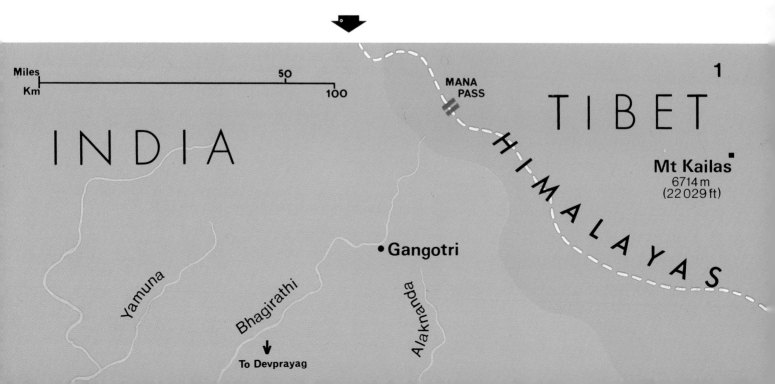

Miles

Km

50

100

MANA
PASS

TIBET

HIMALAYAS

INDIA

Mt Kailas
6714 m
(22 029 ft)

Yamuna

Bhagirathi

To Devprayag

• Gangotri

Alaknanda

This picture of Gangotri was drawn about 100 years ago.
You can see the Hindu temple on the river bank.
There are **rapids** in the river here.
Can you see some waterfalls on the mountains?

Black bears like this one live
in the mountains.

Sheep and goats are kept on the
high pastures.
The shepherds live on milk,
cheese and a kind of porridge.
They also drink tea.
They put salt and butter in
their tea.

Now there is a modern road down the valley from Gangotri.
The road is on the hillside above the deep river gorge.
In the valley there are cedar, pine and spruce trees.

There are also bamboo trees and rhododendron bushes.
Bamboo is used to build shops, market stalls and bridges.

The people of the mountains live in small stone houses.
The houses have thick walls to keep out the winter cold.

Into the Foothills

Here is a farm in the foothills of the Himalayas.
There is a haystack outside each farmhouse.
Can you see the platform with a roof in the field?
This is where children sit to scare birds from the fields.

This is a map of part of the foothills.
Find the town of Devprayag on the map.
This is where the river is first called the Ganges.

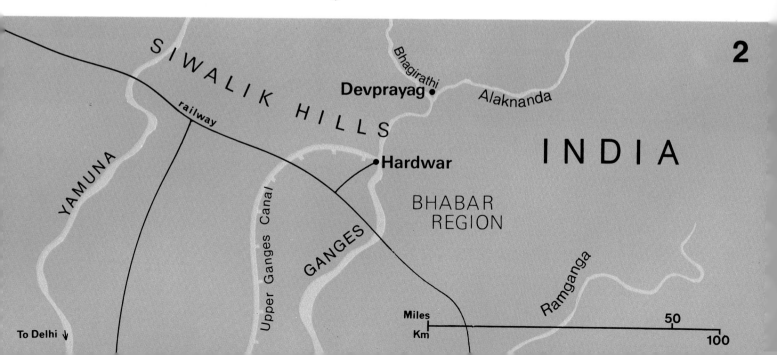

Many trees grow in the
forests here.
Some of them are grown for
their timber.

This tree is called the
Flame of the Forest tree.
How do you think it
got its name?
Its leaves are used to
feed the cattle.

Life in this part of the valley is difficult.
There are landslides on the steep sides of the gorges.
They are caused by heavy rains.
The roads are often blocked by mud and rocks.

Farmers make flat fields in terraces (steps) on the sides of
the hills to stop the soil being washed away by rain.

This is a wild water buffalo.
It is very dangerous.
It lives in swampy ground.
On its back is a bird called a
cattle egret.
There are also jackals,
hyenas, wolves, tigers and
leopards living in the hills.

Peacocks also live here.
Hindus believe that the peacock
is a god on earth.

This is a jungle fowl.
Thousands of years ago our own
chickens were bred from this
kind of wild fowl.

The Gates of Vishnu

The Ganges has dropped steeply down from the mountains
and we have left the hills behind.
Now we shall begin to see many more people.
This is Hardwar, the first large town on our journey.
Here are pilgrims bathing in the river at Hardwar.
The town is a holy place and so it is full of pilgrims.
You can see how crowded the town gets.

This little Indian girl is wearing Western clothes like ours.
Her mother is wearing an Indian **sari**.
She has a **caste mark** on her forehead.

Many pilgrims pay a priest to say prayers for them.
The priests also sell them things they need for worship.
The pilgrims buy scented oil to put on their bodies.
They also buy sandalwood paste to make the caste marks.
Some priests sell garlands of flowers to place on the river.

Here is a street in Hardwar.
The cow goes where it likes.
Cows are sacred to the Hindus
so they must not be harmed.
They cannot be killed for meat.

Most pilgrims stay in cheap
hostels.
They carry their own mattresses
with them.

You cannot eat meat in Hardwar
because it is a holy place.
But there are many vegetarian
restaurants.
The food is cooked in butter.
People drink buttermilk—a
kind of thin yoghurt.

Delhi and the Doab

Many Indian people are poor.
This is how they travel on
the trains.
Some travel on the roof.
Many hang on the outside.
Others sit in the luggage racks.
Sometimes people camp out at a
station and wait for days for
the right train.

New Delhi is the
capital of India.
Find it on the map.
What river is it on?
Find the River Ganges.

3

Delhi

New Delhi

GANGES

YAMUNA

Upper Ganges Canal

Great Trunk Road

DOAB

Agra

Taj Mahal

To Allahabad →

Chambal

Miles
Km
50
100

Here is a shop in Delhi.
The man is selling clothes.
Some are Western style.
Most Indians buy the cloth
to make their own clothes.

The Doab is south of Delhi.
It is a farming area.
The farmers grow cotton,
sugar-cane and oil seed.
The fields are watered by
irrigation.
Water is taken in ditches from
the river to the fields.

Every scrap of land is used.
Cattle graze on paths and the
edges of fields.
Their dung is used for fuel as
there is not much firewood.

Here is the **bazaar** in the old part of Delhi.
It is a busy area full of small shops and stalls.
It is very near the station.

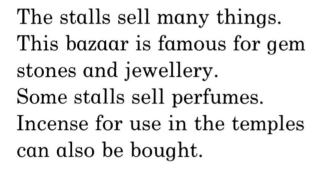

The stalls sell many things.
This bazaar is famous for gem stones and jewellery.
Some stalls sell perfumes.
Incense for use in the temples can also be bought.

You can buy almost anything in the bazaar.
But it is very crowded.
It is very easy to get lost.
Would you like to go there?

Old Delhi was built by
the **Moguls**.
It has city walls and
a huge fortress.

The Moguls built another
fortress south of Delhi
at Agra.
Here is a pavilion inside
the Agra fortress.
The fort stands by the river.
It is built on marshy land
which is full of snakes.

Inside the fort is a **harem**
where the women lived.
They were not allowed to live
in the same rooms as the men.
The women could look out
from this pavilion without
being seen.

This is the Taj Mahal near Agra.
It is one of the most famous buildings in the world.
It was built by a Mogul emperor as a memorial to his wife.

Into the Ganges Plain

In the swampy areas near the river there are tigers.
Tigers do not like hot, dry weather so they enjoy swimming to cool down.

Hardly anyone lives near the river in this area.
The river is full of large boulders.
There are many floods.

Wild animals such as leopards, tigers and wild dogs hide in the tall grass.

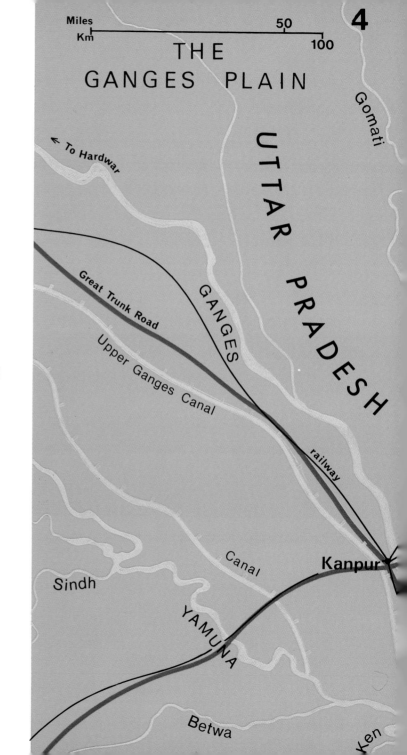

4

Miles

Km

50

100

THE GANGES PLAIN

Gomati

← To Hardwar

UTTAR PRADESH

Great Trunk Road

GANGES

Upper Ganges Canal

railway

Canal

Kanpur

Sindh

YAMUNA

Betwa

Ken

Lower down the river becomes a broad, winding stream.
In winter it is less than a kilometre ($\frac{1}{2}$ mile) wide.
In late summer and autumn the river is in flood.
It grows to a width of 3 kilometres ($1\frac{3}{4}$ miles).
Bridges then have to be made from boats.
The boats are tied together side by side across the river.
The tops are covered with planks and straw to make a road.
The villagers who make the bridges charge people to cross.

When a bridge is built it blocks the way for sailing boats.
Small boats have to be lifted around the bridge.
Large boats pay to have the bridge broken to get through.

Here is the River Ganges near Kanpur.

India was once ruled by Britain.
In the old towns we can still see the parts where the
British used to live.
The summers were too hot for British people.
Many left the Ganges plain in summer for cooler places
in the foothills of the Himalayas.

Allahabad

Allahabad is another holy city on the Ganges.
Can you find it on the map below?
About every twelve years a great festival is held here.
It is called the Kumbh Mela.
Millions of people bathe together in the river.
This is what part of a Kumbh Mela looks like.
In the 1954 festival 500 people were crushed to death
in the crowds.

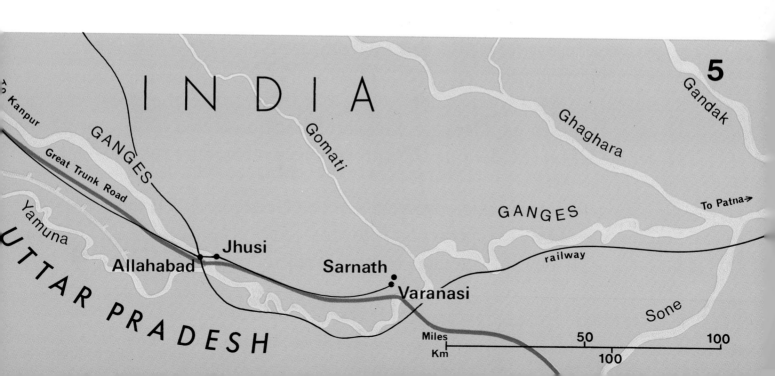

Allahabad was first built by Mogul emperors
more than 400 years ago.
Later the British settled in the city.
They ruled a large part of India from the city.

The British built the railway to Allahabad.
They also built the Great Trunk Road.
This passes through Allahabad on its way from
Delhi to Calcutta.
This road is always full of people.

Pilgrims travel along it to reach the holy cities.
Beggars try to get food and money from them.
Buses travel along it from town to town.
The buses are decorated inside and out with pictures of gods.
Old vans are used as buses for the smaller villages.
The people sit on the floor as the van travels over bumpy roads.

Bullock carts, lorries and cars also use the Great Trunk Road.
The cheapest taxis are pedicabs like this one.
The people sit behind the man on the bike.

In the villages here the houses are made of mud.
The houses are built on mounds of earth to
protect them from floods.
On the banks of the river there are ancient ruined cities.
The easiest way to travel is by boat.
On the way down the river you might see gavials like these.
They are a long-snouted kind of crocodile.

The crocodile above is called a 'mugger'.
It is very hard to see against the rocks.
Muggers can grow to over 3 metres (10 feet) long.
They eat anything, including people.

Vultures live near here and feed on dead animals floating
down the river.

Varanasi, the City of Shiva

These boats and pilgrims are in the city of Varanasi.
It is one of the oldest towns in India and is famous as
a centre for religious teaching.

Varanasi is also a holy city.
Pilgrims make a six-day walk
around the city boundary.
They also have to bathe at
five places on the river and
make offerings to gods.

The bodies of the dead are
burned by the river side.
You can see two bodies on the
steps waiting for **cremation**.

Varanasi is holy to the people who worship the god Shiva. They wear three stripes across their foreheads.
Here is a saddhu (a holy man). He is meditating.
He sits in the lotus position.

Varanasi is famous for silk. Merchants live in big houses where the cloth is made. Some of the cloth has gold thread woven into it.

The city is also noted for work in brass.
This is the bazaar.
You can see brass pots and other things for sale.
Tourists especially like tall vases and small dishes.

Here are washermen at work.
They are called **dhobis**.
They beat the clothes on stones.
When the clothes are clean they
are taken higher up the river
bank and spread out.
The hot sun soon dries them.
Would you like to be a dhobi?

Along the banks of the river
holy men sit in the sun or
shelter under parasols.

There are many temples.
This is the Monkey Temple.
Monkeys live around the water
tank here.
They eat food offered by
pilgrims in the temple.
Many of the temples at Varanasi
are over 1,500 years old.

The leaning temple at Varanasi

From Patna to the Indian Border

The Ganges near Patna is very wide.
When people want to cross the river they use ferry boats.
Here is a crowded ferry boat crossing the river near Patna.

Can you find Patna on this map?

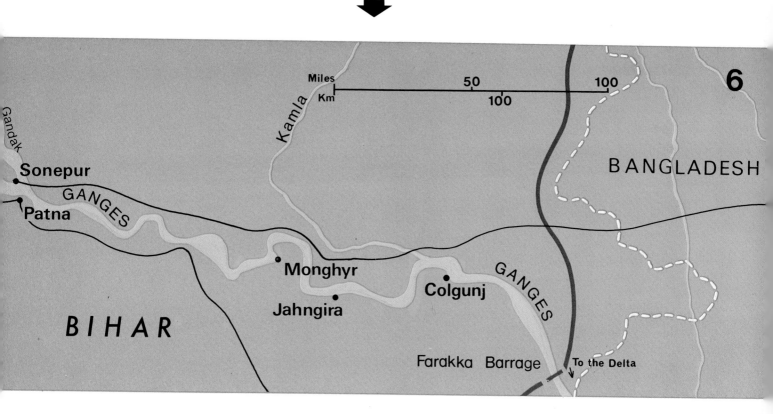

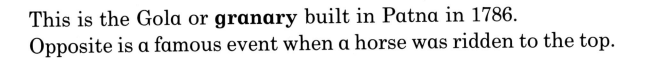

This is the Gola or **granary** built in Patna in 1786.
Opposite is a famous event when a horse was ridden to the top.

49

Rice is grown all over the Ganges Plain around Patna.
Patna rice has long grains and is often served with curries.

Patna is a famous religious centre for the **Sikh** religion.
You may have seen Sikhs—they always wear turbans.

Below Patna there are many old towns on the Ganges.
At Monghyr there is a huge fort built on rocky cliffs.

The river is now very wide.
After the rains the water is
thick and brown with mud.
In times of flood people
climb on to the roofs of
their houses to stay alive.

This picture shows the bends
of the Ganges near Patna.
The photo was taken when
there were floods.
The green fields are paddy
(rice) fields.

These men belonged to the
'Thuggee' sect who lived here
about 150 years ago.
They used to strangle passers-by
and steal their possessions.
They gave what they stole to
the goddess Durga.
One of the English governors
found them out and so the
Thuggee sect was destroyed.
They gave us the word 'thug'.

When the British first settled in India they went to trade.
They formed the East India Company.
This company became very important and powerful.
It brought great wealth to Britain.
Later, Britain ruled over India for many years
until India became independent in 1947.

The Delta

Find three rivers on the map—
the Ganges, the Brahmaputra
and the Meghna.
They carry water into the
Bay of Bengal.
They also drop mud and silt
to form a huge delta.
The delta is in Bangladesh.
This is a new country.
It was founded in 1972.
Most of the people in
Bangladesh are **Muslims**.

Here is the city of Dacca.
It is the chief city in
the delta.
It is the capital city
of Bangladesh.

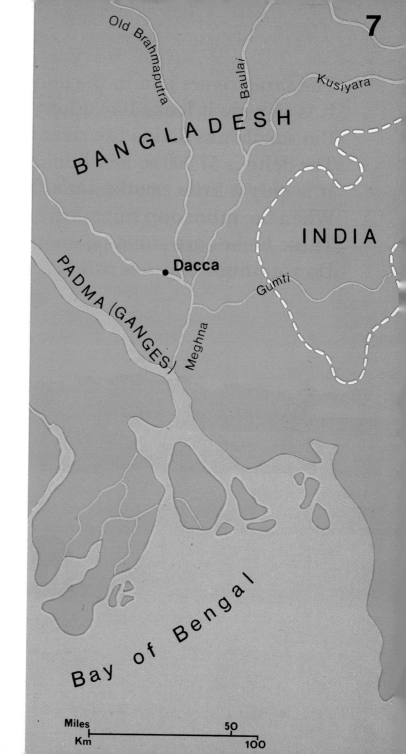

7

The three rivers join in the delta to form the River Padma.
It is so wide it looks like a long lake rather than a river.
Big sandbanks divide the river into many channels.
The delta is 57,000 square kilometres in area (22,000 sq. miles).
It is only a little smaller than the whole of Scotland.
When the **monsoon** rains come the delta becomes a huge lake.
These horses are standing on an island of higher land.
Do you think they are safe?

The floods cover the land
with silt.
The silt is very fertile.
The wetlands are used for
growing rice.
Jute is grown on drier land
to make sacking.

Bangladesh is a very poor
country.
Many people do not have
enough to eat.
Many die in the floods,
or from diseases.
But families are large and the
number of people is growing.

Many poor people in Bangladesh have moved to the cities.
They live in houses made of waste in **shanty towns**.
This man has a job but he earns very little money.

The part of the delta nearest the sea is called
the Sundarbans which means 'beautiful land'.
There are swamps full of tall grasses and reeds
where crocodiles and tigers live.
Some people in the Sundarbans build homes and boats
out of reeds, like those in the picture.

Many people in the delta
have no homes.
This woman is a refugee and
she lives in the drainpipes.

The delta suffers from bad
storms as well as floods.
The storms are called **cyclones**.
Huge waves wash away the soil
and destroy homes.
In 1970 cyclones and tidal
waves killed 600,000 people.

A busy scene at Calcutta docks

Calcutta and the Hooghly

Calcutta is the greatest city
in this part of the world.
It stands at the furthest
point on the River Hooghly
that large ships can reach.
It is a great trading centre.

Dredger boats are used to
keep the port open.
They scoop the silt from
the river channels.

The end of the River Hooghly
is reached at Sagar Island.
This is a holy place
which many pilgrims visit.

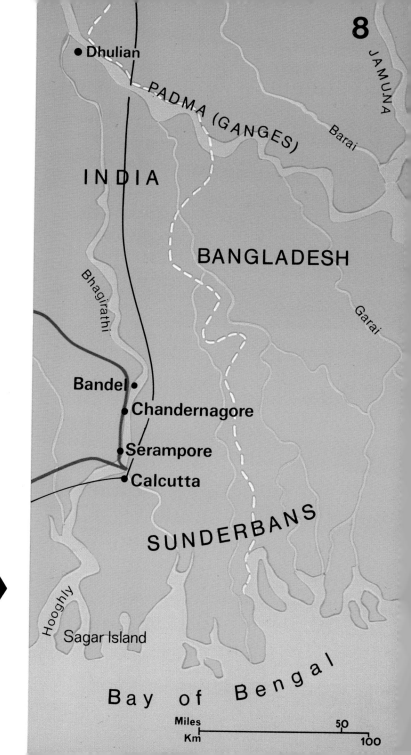

8

Calcutta is bursting with people.
Families live on pavements.
Some use the station as home.
At night there are sleeping
bodies everywhere.
Every night many die from
disease and starvation.
Every morning dead bodies
are collected.
 These people sleep in the street
because they have no homes.

The problems of Calcutta seem too great to solve.
People like Mother Theresa try to help the very poor but
there are more people in need than can be helped.

There is much crime and violence because the city is so crowded.
All the time the number of people in Calcutta grows.

Now the Ganges has reached the end of its journey in the Bay of Bengal.

These people are sailing to the temple on Sagar Island where the river meets the sea.

They will place flower garlands on the water in honour of Ganga, the goddess of the holy River Ganges.

Glossary

Bazaar A market in a town or city in the East.

Caste mark A small mark on the forehead showing which caste a Hindu belongs to.

Castes The classes of society according to the Hindu religion.

Cremation The burning of dead bodies.

Cyclone Storms in which there is heavy rain and very strong winds.

Delta An area of new land which is built up where a river enters the sea.

Dhobi An Indian washerman.

Gorge Very narrow, steep-sided part of a river valley.

Granary A storehouse for grain.

Harem The women's quarters in a Muslim house.

Hindu A follower of an Eastern religion in which many gods are worshipped.

Irrigation Spreading water on to a field to help crops grow.

Mogul   A Muslim ruler of India.

Monsoon   The rains which arrive when winds blow in from the sea in the summer months.

Muslim   A follower of the religion of Islam, based on the teachings of the prophet Mohammed.

Pilgrim   A religious person who travels to a holy place.

Plain   An area of low-lying flat land.

Rapids   A rocky part of a river bed over which the water rushes.

Saddhu   An Indian holy man who has given up the things of the world such as money and possessions and family.

Sari   A dress worn by Indian women, made of a length of cotton or silk wrapped around the body.

Shanty town   Huts and shelters built out of rubbish by homeless people on waste ground at the edges of cities.

Sikhs   A Hindu religious group which believes in only one god.

Silt   Very small pieces of rock and soil carried by a river.

Index

Picture acknowledgements

The illustrations in this book were supplied by: McDougal, Tiger Tops/Ardea 38; Associated Freelance Artists 19 (top); Camerapix Hutchison Library *front cover*; Paul Chinnock 55; Mary Evans 14; Fotofass 9, 42; John Hillelson Agency 8, 12, 58; C. A. R. Hills 23, 28, 29, 40, 43, 50; Keystone 24; Frank Lane 19 (bottom), 30; Lynda Medwell 16, 18, 22, 26, 27, 45; Peter Montagnon *frontispiece*, 21, 34; NHPA 15, 39; Oxfam 54, 56, 60; Ann and Bury Peerless 20, 33, 37, 41, 52, 57, 61; Popperfoto 44 (top and bottom); D. Saunders 10, 46, 48; Wayland Picture Library 49, 51. All other artwork by Alan Gunston.

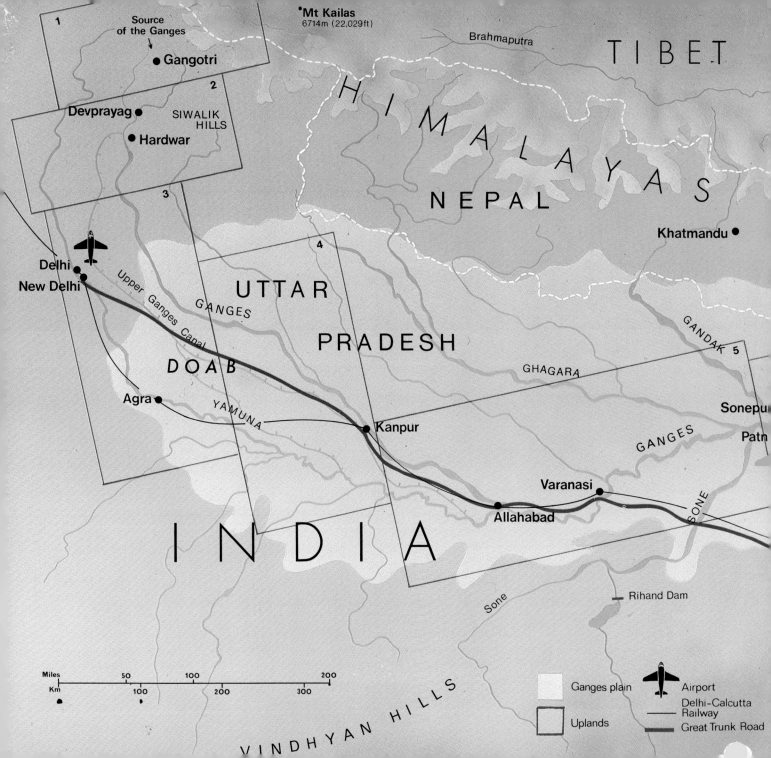